DWAYNE CASPER
Casper's 2nd Journal

IGNORANCE

POVERTY

CLOSED MINDS

lOWSelFesteeM SEPERATION

FEAR HATE

FIGHt tHE FIRE

Written and Illustrated by:
DWIGHT JACKSON

To order additional copies of this book, contact:
Xlibris
844-714-8691
www.Xlibris.com
Orders@Xlibris.com

ISBN: Softcover   978-1-6641-9951-4
        Hardcover   978-1-6641-9952-1
        EBook   978-1-6641-9950-7

Print information available on the last page

Rev. date: 11/19/2021

DWAYNE CASPER

Casper's 2nd Journal

About Me

Seen in new scenes
Livin new life
Subject to means
So saved up my green
And shined up my dreams
An angel from heaven
A demon from hell
Both told me to sail
My soul I wont sell
All the distractions
I had to let go
Channeled the love
Channeled the trust
They came with some life
So I gathered my sins
And brought them to light.
Thank God

Dwight Oneal

&

Co. presents

I Murdered my fears last night.
God I feel free.

LORD, Thank U 4 this 👑 of light 4 all 🔺 did was sacrifice.

The Pyramids Shall Rise Again!

<u>True</u> Kings don't **die**

After dark clouds,

the sun <u>always</u> shines.

9

WENT 2 **WAR** last night

Took shot @ the b3ast

REALIZED

IM A STAR ON MY OWN BEAUTY
FULL OPEN ROAD

HMMM...

LORD KNOWZ

CHAiNz/GANGS V.S. Chaingang

SounDs like the

SaM3 thing

~~YOU DONT HAVE TO BE IN PRISON~~
TO BE ENShackled

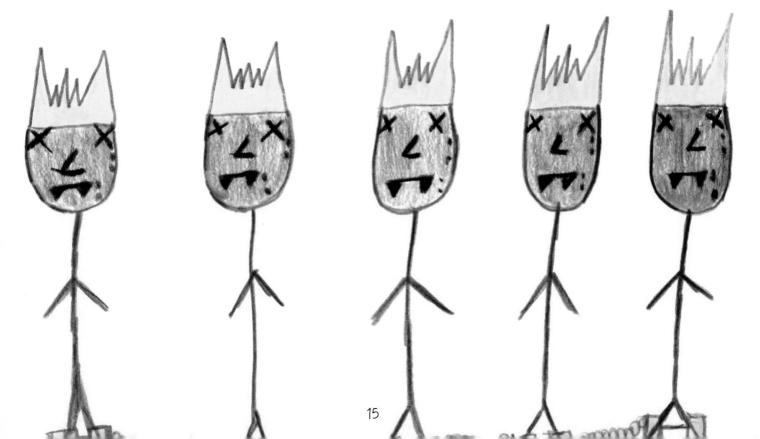

BUT
NO MATTER WHAT,

(REAL) KINGS Still Grow.
TheyRe COMING BACK
FOR EVERYthing & THEY
OWEN.

Printed in the United States
by Baker & Taylor Publisher Services